Meredith is originally from Manhattan, Kansas. She became a registered nurse and now resides in Honolulu, Hawaii. She has always had a passion for poetry and believes that through poetry, one can help heal themselves and others. Besides writing, Meredith spends her time playing in the ocean, hiking with her English Cocker Spaniel named Blue, and traveling as much as possible with her husband, Mark.

For those who dance in the rain.

Meredith Uthoff

GOOD RAIN

AUSTIN MACAULEY PUBLISHERS™

LONDON • CAMBRIDGE • NEW YORK • SHARJAH

Ordering Information
Quantity sales: Special discounts are available on quantity purchases by corporations, associations, and others. For details, contact the publisher at the address below.

Publisher's Cataloging-in-Publication data
Uthoff, Meredith
Good Rain

ISBN 9781685622671 (Paperback)
ISBN 9781685622688 (Hardback)
ISBN 9781685622701 (ePub e-book)
ISBN 9781685622695 (Audiobook)

Library of Congress Control Number: 2023906949

www.austinmacauley.com/us

First Published 2023
Austin Macauley Publishers LLC
40 Wall Street, 33rd Floor, Suite 3302
New York, NY 10005
USA

mail-usa@austinmacauley.com
+1 (646) 5125767

Thank you to all my friends and family. You have inspired me and supported me in all your own unique ways. I am so thankful to have you in my life.

A special thank you to Libby Stratton for always being my biggest cheerleader in all things.

Corbin Campbell, for your poetry challenges and for holding me accountable.

Ingrid Middleton, for encouraging me to follow my dreams and reminding me that I can do it.

Mark Evenson, my loving husband, reminds me daily that anything is possible, especially together.

The Treadmill

I woke up one day and just couldn't do it anymore.
I was tired of feeling like life was a chore.
From deep within I knew it was time to fight,
living a life that just didn't feel right.
I remember myself as a little girl,
dancing in the rain and pondering the world.
Anything was possible.
All my dreams could come true.
Anything I wanted I had the power to do.
Climb the highest mountain.
Be Indiana Jones.
I would be an archeologist and dig up some bones.
One day I was a pilot,
the next a circus act.
In my mind, there was no questioning.
These were just facts.
I didn't worry about money,
or having a fancy car.
Who had the time when I was busy being a star?
I don't know what really happened.
I blinked and was an adult.
I'd really like to know,
because it's obviously someone's fault.

I jumped on this treadmill of school, work, and life.
Feeling pushed to be a success,
be desirable,
become a wife.
I ran on the treadmill for years and years and years,
afraid to get off because of all my silly societal fears.
But I've reached my limit.
I can't run anymore.
I can feel it in my bones,
down to my core.
So I'm going to step off and find a different road,
put it all down,
lighten the load.
The path is not clear.
There may be growing pains,
but I want to find that girl who dances in the rain.

Kansas

Jumping on hay bales,
climbing some trees,
trying to be a big girl
when I get stung by a bee.
Dance in the garden,
it smells of fresh earth.
I pick berries with Grandma,
she calls me strawberry girl.
She had a Mona Lisa smile,
so soft and so kind.
There was something more there
but hard to define.
I rode grandpa's horses and
swam in the creek.
Took a three-year break
after I got my first leech.
Talking to the chickens
and chasing their peeps.
My favorite thing was feeding
all those baby sheep.
Imaginary adventures deep in the forest.
I'd steal from the rich
and give to the poorest.

Lightning bugs on a warm summer's night,
mimic the stars with their tiny night lights.
Looking up to the moon,
in the trees I sit.
Listening to the cicadas one last time before they split.
No matter where I travel, or how far I roam,
I will always remember:
There is no place like home.

Surfer Girl

Surfer Girl
She knows how to party,
shows up just in time to be fashionably tardy.
Sea Salt
Smile on her face
You know the one who's always setting the pace.
Wind-swept hair
She dances with the surf.
You better keep up if you play on her turf.
Surfer girl has a fire in her heart.
She charges the waves and
makes the sea part.

Kangaroo

If I was an animal,
I'd be a kangaroo.
I'd put you in my pocket,
and this is what we'd do:
I'd jump you to the mountains
and hop you to the sea.
I'd take you any place
that you would want to be.

My Love

I love you more than the sun,
who lights my path and warms my buns.
I love you more than the moon and stars,
who conjure my dreams of travels afar.
I love you more than the deep blue sea,
whose depth and knowledge set me free.
I love you more than the mountaintops,
whose peaks and valleys never stop.
Sometimes what will be shall be,
like the sun and the moon,
the stars and the sea.
Just remember, if you ever start to fall,
my love for you conquers them all.

Little Bit

I gave a little bit of my heart here and there,
for all the ones that I do care.
I gave a little bit of my heart to you,
because my feelings were so true.
But as I was giving my heart to thee,
I forgot to keep a little heart for me.
So even though I search far and wide,
I only feel my heart with you by my side.

Purple and Pink

Purple and pink
sometimes make you sink
into thoughts and dreams unknown.
So if you have a dream
that you wish would come true,
I'll meet you where the pink turns into the blue.

Odds

What are the odds that I would be me?
A number bigger than fish in the sea?
What are the odds that you would be you?
A number greater than the stars that shine true?
And what are the odds that we would meet?
And that each other's company would feel like a treat?
A million? A billion? Infinity plus?
I feel like this is more than just lust.
I'm drawn to you like lightning rods.
So I'm asking you:
Will you take the odds?

My Orchid

My orchid has a beautiful face,
with wild pink lips and
pure white petals made of lace.
Fuchsia freckles speckle the petals of white snow.
Reminds me of my childhood face
that I no longer know.

Restless Heart

A restless heart.
A wondering mind.
With a little adventure
I will be fine.
With so much to see
and so much to do.
To stay in one place
would make me feel blue.

What If

What if we threw away all the couldn'ts and cannots,
the shouldn'ts, the wouldn'ts, the haven'ts and have nots?
What if we let go of all the excuses for a time?
Maybe live in a world where the biggest problem
is what is going to rhyme?
What if I said to you all the things I wanted to say?
Would you stand your ground?
Turn around?
Or simply run away?
I've caught a shooting star,
danced on mountains near and far.
I've seen molten lava flow from earth,
but I still continued the search.
So I swam with turtles in the sea,
met some sharks who didn't mess with me.
I laid in a rainbow,
climbed a moss-covered tree.
But time and time again,
when I look at you and me,
I can't help but wonder,
what if?

Dear Stranger

They say dream big and shoot for the stars,
but most days I feel like I'm already on Mars.
I don't know your journey,
or how far you've come.
All I know is we both rest under the same setting sun.
So dear stranger, that I have never met,
wipe your brow and don't you fret.
I know this is a weird thing to do,
but I wanted you to know
that I'm rooting for you.

Stuck

I feel stuck today.
I just don't know what to do.
I know that it will pass,
that this feeling won't last.
But I feel waist-deep in goo,
like I have lead in my shoe.
I'm craving something new,
but what that is I have no clue.
So I'm just waiting, feeling blue.
Do you at times feel like that too?

The Great Mermaid Escape

I met a mermaid today with long golden hair.
She summoned me to swim into her lair.
After I dove into her caverns of blue,
my rose-colored glasses had a change of hue.
The mermaid pushed a boulder in front of my only escape;
instead of a friendly swim, I was going to end up on her
plate!
But I wasn't going to give up on this quite strange plight,
so I grabbed some starfish and got ready for a ninja
throwing fight!
But the starfish only stunned her,
and the next thing that I knew,
I was tied up with an octopus,
that's when I knew that I was through.
As the mermaid was getting ready to sample my favorite
toes,
I was able to grab a trumpet fish and shove it up her nose.
As the mermaid struggled to release the fish from her
head,
she thought to herself:
I should've never gotten up from my comfy seaweed bed.
She was devastated; she was beat by only a mere mortal.

She will rue the day she ever let me deep inside her porthole.

Space Dust

We are all particles of tiny space dust,
set free on this Earth,
but not destined to rust.
The more you travel,
the more you can see
that I could be you
and you could be me.

Dreaming

I dreamed about you last night.
We packed a bag and took a flight
to a faraway land.
I'm not sure of the place.
But man,
it was so good to see your face.

S3

Sun, Surf, and Salt.
I fell in love and it wasn't my fault.

Highs and Lows

The highest highs and the lowest lows.
You are the only one that knows,
just where you are and where you've been,
and how quickly the world seems to spin.
So close your eyes and take a breath,
because my friend, you deserve a rest.
From the highest highs and the lowest lows.
It is what it is...
I suppose.

Sail Away

A thousand miles across the sea,
we could meet in the middle and have some tea.
On a sailboat, we could be free,
for you to be you and me to be me.
Hold me close as we rock to sleep,
in the middle of the ocean,
the secrets of the deep.
Then tell me everything is alright,
as we sail away into the starry night.

Power

What if I told you that you have the power to create?
To make your life full of the good and the great?
There is magic deep in your heart.
To release it, all you have to do is start.

Tiny Bubbles

Tiny bubbles under the sea,
with my breath I set you free.
With an underwater giggle, you tickle my face.
Tiny bubbles made up of water lace.
I watch you dance in beams of light,
with rainbow fish and turtles in sight.
I watch you float to the world on top,
a world that always ends in a POP!
But don't feel bad for the bubbles you see,
because the magic of bubbles lives in me.

Underwater Waltz

At sharks cove we took a chance,
so under water we did dance.
Secret caverns fifty feet under sea,
no one around, just you and me.
You took my hand and held me close,
and this was the part that I loved the most:
I looked deep in your eyes through tempered glass,
I felt the future and let go of the past.
Spinning around the cavern,
I could feel the music in my heart.
Then just when I thought it couldn't get more romantic…
I had an underwater fart.

Good Rain

As the sky turned gray and the sun wouldn't shine,
I came to the realization that you would never be mine.
The clouds grew heavy with sadness and tears.
From the look of the sky, it would never clear.
Finally, the clouds couldn't take any more,
so they opened up and down they poured.
They filled up the ocean, the rivers, and lakes.
A reflection of my heart that continues to ache.
But the rain will stop and the sun will shine,
and once again I will be fine.
No need to hang on to sadness and pain.
Sometimes the soul just needs a good rain.

Smile

If they told me the only way I could stay
was losing bits of myself along the way,
I'd take a knife and cut off piece by piece,
because I know this body is just on lease.
Until one day there will be nothing left.
Just kindly place my smile with the rest.

Present

I fell in love with the future
while regretting the past,
missing the present that was flying by fast.

Goodbyes

I'm going to let you go,
because there is nothing left to do.
At the end of the day, I just want you to be you.
Although it makes me sad
to see you walk away.
I know it would hurt even more
if I asked for you to stay.
Although this chapter is done,
our books are not complete.
Who knows where we are going,
what we are doing,
or who we are going to meet?
In the end, I want to thank you
for all that we have shared.
Sometimes two puzzle pieces just
don't quite fit when they are paired.

Hello Nurse

Stop the bleeding,
take away the pain,
prevent infection,
comfort the insane.
Kiss all the booboos,
clean up some poo.
These are just some things
that I frequently do.

Revolution

In a world of violence, hate and war,
poverty, illness, starvation and more,
unjust persecution, politics, and pollution,
we want to stay focused on the solution,
to stand up and finally start a revolution!
But every day a new headline blares,
and most days you wonder if anyone truly cares.
Wanting to help but not knowing what steps to take.
What kind of future are we going to make?
It is time to raise up and let our voices be heard.
Love is the answer for hatred to be cured.
Deep down we all know what needs to come to fruition.
We can no longer give excuses for this human condition.

Muse of Pain

Maybe you aren't my love.
Maybe you are my muse of pain.
Something that makes it rain.
A river of tears to form a path
so that all the grief can
leave my body at last.
To find a way out.
It's not just the pain of losing you.
It's the feelings of abandonment,
unworthiness,
fear.
Let me be clear:
Things I've buried deep below that
the streams could never touch to wash away are now
flooded,
flowing,
releasing.
Although I feel like at times I am drowning
and I can't hold my breath,
I'm going to choose to float down this stream of misery.
I give up all control.
I don't know where it is taking me,
but for the first time I am free.

Mere the Bear

I'm going to tell you a story of a girl named Mere,
who tried to teleport to her sister
but instead got turned into a bear.
The calculations were double-checked,
the engineering complete.
Just a couple wires got mixed up and
failed to connect where they were supposed to meet.
As Mere confidently threw the lever,
she felt a tingle in her toes.
She knew something wasn't quite right
when a faint smell of honey crept into her nose.
And ZAAAAPP!!!
Just like that,
she was suddenly a bear!
She thought to herself,
Wow! I have a lot of hair!
Of course, Mere's sister was devastated
that her loved one was a beast,
but she vowed to make the best of things,
and instead of moping,
made a feast.
There were pounds of bright red berries,
a large assortment of fresh fish.

All the delicacies that any bear could wish for,
every single dish.
So Mere the bear ate and ate and ate.
She ate so much not a single scrap was
left upon her plate.
Then Mere got real tired,
it was time to hibernate.
So she found a cozy cave,
told herself to be brave.
She closed her eyes,
took a deep breath,
then she slept a sleep that looked a lot like death.
Then with a flutter of eye lashes,
the morning sun crept in.
Mere's arms and legs felt like needles and pins.
With a stretch, Mere opened her eyes,
she let out a sigh of relief and surprise!
She was back in her body,
in her own bed!
The whole thing was a dream that she made up in her
head.
She jumped up to call her sister to send her birthday
wishes,
but as she opened her mouth, she burped…
and could only smell fishes.

Rape

Well, what was she wearing?
Did she have too much to drink?
Did she do anything to entice him?
He wouldn't do that…. I don't think.
I heard that she was crazy.
I heard she only wants revenge.
I heard she's just a really big slut.
I feel sorry for the man.
Is this even worth it?
I mean it's water under the bridge.
Is there any chance she's lying?
Even a little bit?
Even a smidge?
After all, there's a man's reputation at stake,
should we ruin his life for just one mistake?
Boys are boys who can't help their sexual thirst.
Besides, it's not like she was even the first.

Machu Picchu

Machu Picchu of Peru
So many wonders but I choose you.
Alpacas roam your mountaintops,
breathtaking views that make you stop.
Remnants of ancient civilization remain.
Whispers of alien help sound insane.
There you stand in all your glory,
but the Incas are the only ones
that can tell your full story.

White Flies

White flies around my hibiscus plant,
I hate you more than my infestation of ants.
You choke the life leaf by leaf,
with your milky-white powder you release.
To my plants, you are nothing but a leech.
And with this poem I do beseech:
Please halt your actions of pure tyranny,
and restore my garden to joyous tranquility.

Goo

I am dirt, mud, and sweat.
I am the primordial goo that has
pulled itself out of the darkness.
To breathe that first breath that ignites
the fire within my belly.
I have come from nothing and yet
I am everything all at once.
I don't blame those that look away.
Just as one cannot stare into the sun,
to come eye to eye with such power
can be blinding.

A Far-Off Place

A shooting star.
A candle wish.
From a far-off land there came a kiss.
I sent it on a turtle's shell,
across the ocean it knows so well.
A starfish then tickled it free,
but it was promptly picked up by a bee
who flew it home to turn into honey,
hoping he was going to make some money.
But a grizzly bear set it free,
trying to find some honey for his tea.
Then a meadowlark scooped it up,
because he wanted to give it to a pup.
That pup's name was Gus, you see,
and he knew just where that kiss should be.
So don't mind Gus if he licks your face,
its's just a kiss from a far-off place.

Sisters

Sacred sisters sit and spill secrets
of spiritual awakenings under the waterfall mist.
The magic in these words wrap around me
like the green moss hugging the wet stones.
The water droplets fall in the never-ending cycle
that is life.

More

I love you,
but I want to love me more.
Because maybe then my heart
won't be so sore.

Walking

I'm walking down the street,
moving to my own beat,
when suddenly a strange man appears,
and from deep within swell up all my fears.
He's drawn to my light like a moth to a flame,
a person with a mind that is untamed.
I try to tell myself that I'm not going to die,
but he's got that look of meth in his eye.
My heart is pounding out of my chest,
this is not just a harmless pest.
Last second he turns when I make eye contact.
And I feel like a fly that's been released from a trap.
It shouldn't feel like a death-defying feat.
I'm just a woman trying to walk down the street.

The Last Time

I can still feel your fingers in my hair.
The electricity that runs through my body
as you pull me in closer to breathe me in.
Lips almost touching.
Torturing, teasing pleasure.
Time stops and the world melts around us.
I never want to leave.

Dating

Am I too much?
Not good enough to date,
but good enough to touch?
When I set my sights on you,
I never really had a clue,
who I was or what I deserved.
All my love was on reserve.
I gave it all.
Yet it was not enough.
This dating thing is really rough.

I Am Big Love

I am adventure and ideas.
I am travel, magic, music, and art.
I am hiking and nature.
A waterfall.
A good hug.
I am the spirit
restless,
willing,
waiting
and wondering.
I am a lot but I am not too much.
I am what I am at the exact time I am supposed to be.
I am here for a reason,
even if I don't know exactly what that reason is.
I am here.
I am big love.

Free

Late night epiphany
only good things are meant for me.
There are galaxies in my head.
This is the end of existential dread.
Love is all there is to be.
Now I'll let my soul feel free.

Cheers

Cheers to all my badass bitches,
to the spirit guides, the star seeds,
and the spellbound witches.
To the fairies, sprites, and even the gnomes.
Talking to you feels like coming home.

Glimmers

I see glimmers of a love so true,
a love more powerful than the moon.
I see it in your eyes,
I feel it in your touch,
but you run away when you feel too much.
And as I recite my love poetry to thee,
there is never any love poetry for me.
I've waited with patience.
I've waited with class.
But maybe all you wanted was just some ass.
And glimmers are lovely in their own right.
But it's the glimmers that keep me up late at night.

Flying

Cotton candy clouds
Like a fresh snow
Early morning
Flying high above
Feel the sun on my face
I'm in heaven.

Hospice

Electrons and neutrons deep within my cells
are vibrating at a higher rate,
surely, you can tell?
I can feel something big coming,
I just don't know what it is.
Please hold my hand while I take
life's final quiz.

I'm a Rainbow

I am a rainbow on a cloudy day.
I am the friend that reminds you to play.
I am the breeze when it's stagnant outside.
I am the treasure that washed up with the tide.
I am the giggle that escaped from the lips.
I am the one that caught you when you slipped.
And when I'm feeling down and out,
I remember I'm these things and more to count.

Gardening Advice

I planted a garden.
It's been growing for years.
It's been made from all the laughs,
every tear, every fear.
I planted a garden.
I admit it has some weeds,
that's just because I didn't tend to all its needs.
I planted a garden and it's colorful and unique.
Every year I find myself thinking that it's finally starting
to peak.
So as you plant your garden,
don't judge it harshly day by day,
for every single garden starts as a tiny pot of clay.

Quest

On my quest to discover self-love,
a mission for my soul I sent from above.
All the trials and tribulations from this life and past
set me on a path to conquer this task.
Up to this point, I've been holding my breath.
A fish out of water, afraid of death.
Then I realized something I learned in a dream:
That I don't need to swim upstream.
I'm going to let it flow, dance in sun beams.
My inner child just wants to be seen.
And in the present, I found some peace.
My soul is forever, the body on lease.
My quest is a journey.
It will take time.
But at least I know,
I'll forever be mine.

The Camel's Back

You were not the straw that
broke the camel's back.
You were the straw that
helped me realize I can carry
so much more.

To Be Loved

You say you want to be loved…
But I have climbed the highest mountain and
declared my love for you in no uncertain terms
only to be met back by an echo of my own voice.
I try to hold my grip firmly at the top because I know in
my heart it is you that belongs at the peak with me,
breathing in the crisp air of the dawn as the sun breaks
through the clouds.
But the ice is melting and my foot is starting to slip.
I can't make you climb that mountain,
maybe you are scared of heights.
But maybe I don't want to be with someone who isn't
willing to fight.
You say you want to be loved,
but I've been here this whole damn time.
You don't know how to climb a mountain?
Start with one step and take your time.

The End of the World

It was suffering a million little deaths.
I would mourn you, grieve for you,
ugly sob into my pillow night after night,
until it felt like there was nothing left…
Only to awaken in the morning to a small breadcrumb
you had left for me while the world was ending.
I would hungrily devour the tiny morsel
because I was starving for your love.
Even that tiny morsel was enough to bring me back to
life…
Only to die again the following night.

Just Float

A sparkle of water
A glimmer of light
There are moments in life
where the timing feels right.
So when the storm hits
and you can't find your boat,
don't forget that you
yourself can float.

The One

They only want you to want them.
They need you to love them.
As I sat and admired his nice suit
made out entirely of red flags,
I thought to myself:
He could be the one.
It was in that moment I realized I have always loathed
myself my whole life.
I wish I had given myself a small piece of the compassion
I had shown my narcissists.
So eager to be the sacrificial lamb. Almost to the point
they probably could not NOT treat me poorly. I was
subconsciously begging them to abuse me. So did my
narcissist make me the way I am or did I mold my
narcissist into a narcissist? Did I ruin everyone's life by
manifesting what I thought I deserved?
But now that you see,
you don't have to do that anymore.
You can forgive yourself and start giving yourself the love
that you not only want but that you truly deserve.

Bike Ride Day

As I rode my bike, I thought of you,
and for the first time that didn't make me feel blue.
I hoped that you were doing okay,
that you were making time to laugh and play,
that your world was bright with sun not rain,
and that you weren't in any pain.
Since I let you go and you had nothing to say,
now you're just a thought on a bike ride day.

M&M

You took me off guard one sunny day.
We were just friends who were going to play.
I looked into your eyes and I fell hard.
Could this be a love that was written in the stars?
We daydream of adventures in faraway lands,
my partner in crime,
finding treasures in the sand.
I don't know the future,
sometimes I don't know what to say....
All I know is that
"we will get there someday."

Love Birds

Two birds met in the zoo.
They fell in love and that love grew.
Their love grew so big it couldn't fit in the cage.
That's when the birds knew it was time for a change.
So that next morning,
at sunrise,
they took the zookeeper
by surprise.
When he wasn't looking, they made their escape.
No turning back.
Their love was at stake.
They flew in sun.
They flew in rain.
They flew in weather that seemed insane.
They had many adventures and their love grew more.
When you escape, you don't know what's in store.
They only wish that everyone knew
that you too can escape from your zoo.

The Voice

I'm in love
and I'm terrified.
I want to sit back and enjoy the ride.
But there is a voice deep inside
that says:
"What if it's all a lie,
and one day he's going to tell you goodbye
and once again you will be left to cry."
And then I worry I might just die!
Then he looks at me with his deep blue eyes,
holds me close and lets me cry,
kisses each tear as it rolls down my face,
assures me my love isn't misplaced.
This isn't the same story I've read before.
I'm scared because it is so much more.
I want to put my mind to rest.
I simply want to manifest.
A love that I truly deserve.
A love that I don't have to grade on a curve.
I found my love
at long last.
Now I just need to let go of the past.

Grandmother

My grandmother painted a picture
of a place that she never did see.
And even though I never met her,
I think she manifested this for me.

All the Colors

I am red fading into a fiery orange.
I am a little yellow in the eye of the storm.
I'm a little green like the rebirth of spring.
On days when I feel like I'm living a dream.
I'm a calm blue while I'm lying next to you.
On a rainy day with nothing else to do.
I'm a little violet when I'm feeling shy.
Not every single rainbow is high up in the sky.